MW01613507

"Th
discer
stand on faith, values, and more."

Brian R. Barcaro
Co-Founder, CatholicMatch.com
Pittsburgh, Pennsylvania

"This is one of those books that make you go hmmmmmmm. Perfect topics for dinner time. It should be on the desk of every youth minister."

Brian Shields
Producer, Therese, the movie
Jacksonville, Florida

"Dominic does it again! Fantastic questions for basic "get-to-know-me" info, for fun and the very in-depth things people ought to know about each other when developing relationships, be they business, friendship, or romance. Order me a case of these to hand out at concerts!"

Annie Waugh
Catholic recording artist and entertainer
Bolingbrook, Illinois

"Dominic Catalano is a charismatic kind of guy who loves his faith and lets it show! His special gift is energizing young adults, and it is his openness and enthusiasm for the Church which draws them to him. The format of this book will be especially appealing to all ages and will encourage discussion at all levels."

Mary Ann Kuharski
Director, Prolife Across America "The Billboard People",
www.ProLifeAcrossAmerica.org
Minneapolis, Minnesota

"It is not only important to know our Catholic faith, but to grow in our Catholic faith. This book pushes you to think about where you stand, how you feel, who you want to be, and what it means to be a Catholic in today's world."

Beth Burwell
Student, University of Central Florida
Orlando, Florida

"Conversation! This lost art could use a boost...or 200+ boosts! The questions are a great spark for delightful, challenging, intriguing conversation."

Kathy Donohue
Teacher, San Miguel School
Chicago, Illinois

"What a great tool for personal growth and for relationships at all levels. Discover what your faith really means to you and to others—as you engage in the dynamic and fun conversations that will surely follow from QUESTIONS FOR CATHOLICS. These questions cover the spectrum of life experience for Catholic Christians and provide a great way to keep your Catholic faith at the heart of all your relatioships."

Carmen Marcoux
Author of Catholic courtship novel, Arms of Love
Saskatoon, Saskatchewan, Canada

Questions
For
Catholics

Questions
For
Catholics

Growing
Relationships
One Question
At A Time

Dominic Catalano

ISBN: 1-889465-08-9

CATprints
Post Office Box 441
Eustis, Florida 32727-0441
www.eCATgear.com

Printed in the United States of America

Book Production: SPS Publications,
Eustis, Florida (www.spsbooks.com)
Book and Cover Design: Mollie Johanson

DEDICATION

———————— ◆ ————————

To my my nieces and nephews…

Nicholas, Benjamin, Samantha, Olivia,
Joshua, Madelaine, Christina, McKinley,
Jack, Annabelle, Kurt, and Kaitlin

for all the questions…
Keep asking!

INTRODUCTION

I've always asked lots of questions, especially when dealing with people. When I was younger, asking questions was a way to find out about others. As I've gotten older, I've been able to learn more about myself. The classroom of life is truly in the asking AND the answering.

This book is a product of the desire to know about myself as well as to know more about others. Some friends have suggested a section with ANSWERS according to the Catholic Church. Maybe this will be part of a future book, but for now I encourage you to grab a Catechism of the Catholic Church and investigate for yourself. Remember that the Catechism has input from Sacred Scripture and the early Church Fathers, so it's loaded with information. Also, there are thousands of sites on the web that will help you discover truth, and I recommend starting with the Vatican's website, www.Vatican.va.

So grab your Catechism, break open QUESTIONS FOR CATHOLICS, and start asking questions. This book is great for small group discussions, dating, family forums, icebreakers, and much more. Enjoy!

Pax!

Dominic Catalano

Dominic Catalano
Eustis, Florida

p. s. Perhaps one of your questions could be used in a future QUESTIONS FOR CATHOLICS or you'd like to share how this book has helped you. If so, then we'd like to hear from you. Send me an email at Dominic@eCATgear.com or mail me at the following address:

Dominic Catalano
c/o CATprints
Post Office Box 441
Eustis, Florida 32727-0441
attn: Questions for Catholics

1

What is your favorite part about being Catholic?

MASS. RECEIVING COMMUNION

2

Who is your favorite saint
and why?

ELIZABETH SETON -

SUCH A GOOD MOTHER, TEACHER,
WIFE.

ST. FRANCIS -

ACTIONS SPOKE VOLUMES

3

Which mystery of the
Rosary best exemplifies
your life right now?

NOW AND FOR YEARS —
THE JOYFUL MYSTERIES.

* MARY'S JOY WHEN JESUS
CAME INTO THE WORLD.

4

Who is your favorite
person in the Bible and
why?

5

What does Paul mean when he writes "the pillar and foundation of truth is the church" in 1 Timothy 3:15?

6

Are you a Martha or a Mary?

7

What would Jesus drive?

SOMETHING UNDERSTATET -
IF ANYTHING AT ALL.

8

What's your favorite Bible verse and why?

9

How can you apply "Catholicism is not a spectator sport" to your life?

10

Where do you see yourself in five years?

11

What is a show stopper for
you in any relationship?

DISHONESTY

12

Are you closer to your mom or your dad? Why?

13

Where did your family go
on vacation?

CALIFORNIA

14

How do you bounce back
from a bad day?

PRAYER AND OPTIMISM

15

What book are you reading right now?

THIS ONE... :)

THOMAS MERTON

THE SEVENTH STOREY MOUNTAIN

16

What do you think about when you think of Jesus's mother, Mary?

17

Did you see Mel Gibson's movie, THE PASSION OF THE CHRIST? What are your thoughts on the movie?

18

What part of the Mass do you like the best and why?

COMMUNION.

THE GIFT OF SPIRITUAL LIFE.

19

If you could travel any-
where in the world with
time and money not
being factors, where
would you go?

ITALY/ROME

TO SEE ALL THE BEAUTIFUL
                    CHURCHES.

20

What do you remember
most about Mass as a kid?

WATCHING COMMUNION
BEING TAKEN.

21

What different smells
remind you of church?

THE SMELL OF CANDLES,
INSCENTS

22

Which song at Mass is
your favorite?

GLORY TO GOD IN
THE HIGHEST ♫

23

If you had to describe the Eucharist to a nine year old kid, how would you do it?

24

When you do well on something, with whom do you share it?

ONLY GOD USUALLY

25

Do you like singing during
Mass or not? Why?

YES! IT JUST FEELS
GO RIGHT/GOOD.

26

Should crying babies stay
in church during Mass?

No

27

What do you think of when you say "Lord, I am not worthy to receive you, but only say the word and I shall be healed"?

28

When was the last time
you went to confession?

2 WEEKS AGO

29

When was the last time
you cried? What made
you cry?

YESTERDAY,

WHEN MY KIDS WERE
GOING TO LEAVE.

30

---•---

What part of weddings
do you like the most?
the least?

31

Why do people spend so
much on weddings?

FOR THE GUESTS!!

32

What do you think causes
infidelity in marriages?
How can they be avoided?

33

What is your favorite prayer?

OUR FATHER...

HAIL MARY

34

Describe yourself in
one word.

RESILIANT

35

Where do you see yourself
in 10 years?

36

What does the story of
the Good Samaritan mean
to you?

37

What part(s) of the
Catholic faith cause
you the most struggle?

38

Can you name the twelve apostles?

39

Who is the priest who has
influenced you the most
in your faith journey?

FATHER RICK

FATHER WILLIAM

40

Have you ever had a
moment when you felt
God was speaking to you?

41

Do you find it easy to
forgive and forget?

42

When Jesus was on the cross, what caused Him the most pain?

43

How do you recommend that today's teens live a chaste life?

44

What does chastity mean to you?

45

---•---

How can you get more
involved in your church?

46

If you could give your
parish priest feedback
on how to improve your
church, what would it be?

47

What role would a
spiritual director play
in your life?

48

Which version of the Ave Maria do you prefer?

49

What geographical
names in your area have
been influenced by the
Catholic faith? (ex. St.
Charles, Maryland, etc.)

St. Louis

50

What does dressing
modestly mean to you?

51

If you could speak a
foreign language which
one would it be?

GAELIC

52

What does is mean to be pro-life?

53

What does it mean to be pro-choice?

54

What person has influenced you the most in your faith walk? How so?

55

Have you ever considered
the religious life as a priest,
deacon, brother, or sister?

YES!

I WANTED TO BE A

NUN.

56

What are your thoughts
on adoption?

ITS LIFE SAVING

57

What does love mean
to you?

58

What would you want
someone to say about you
after you die?

THAT I HAD A GOOD
HEART.

59

Which book has helped you the most in your faith journey? How so?

60

If you could change anything in the Catholic church, what would it be?

A CLOSER WATCH ON
PRIESTS REGARDING
CHILD ABUSE

61

Is fashion today more modest or less? How would you change it?

62

How would you improve
social justice with all in
your community?

63

What has changed
about modesty in your
generation as compared
to modesty in your
parents' generation?

WOMEN + GIRLS WEAR
A LOT LESS!

64

You can invite three world leaders to dinner, who would they be and why?

65

How do you understand purgatory?

66

What's your Catholic
periodical of choice?

67

How can Mass be seen as a healing agent?

68

What law could be passed that would help strengthen the family?

69

What does sin look like
to you?

70

What can you change to improve your prayer life?

71

How do you pray?

72

When was the last time
you prayed the Rosary?

73

How can you be more like Mary and bear Christ to your world?

74

---•---

Who is your favorite
priest and why?

75

Have you ever been on a retreat? If so, what was it like?

76

Which is worse, drinking
or smoking? Why?

77

Why didn't Jesus include women in the Twelve Apostles?

78

Have you ever been on a
church mission trip? If
so, where did you go and
what did you do?

79

Do you support a charity?
If so, which one?

80

Should teens date one on one or in groups? Why?

81

How can older folks be more tolerant of teens in today's church?

82

How can teens be more tolerant of older folks in today's church?

83

When the priest says "this is My body and this is My blood," do you believe it? Why or why not?

84

How do you prepare for
Mass?

85

Can you name some famous people who are practicing Catholics?

86

How could Hollywood better portray the Catholic church in the movies?

87

Should the United States have sent troops into Iraq? Why or why not?

88

How can you apply
the story of the Good
Samaritan in your life?

89

Which is your favorite
bible story? Why?

90

What was the most profound experience that you've ever had at a Pro-Life march or event? Where was it and what was it like?

91

How would you explain
God to an agnostic?

92

If God was a musical
instrument which one
would He be? Why?

93

If you were a musical instrument which one would you be? Why?

94

If you could play an instrument, which one would you play?

95

How can you get more in-
volved in the Sacraments?

96

A man can not afford the medical care for his ailing wife. Is it okay for him to steal the medicine in order to help cure her?

97

How do you deal with conflict?

98

If you could tell a story about your grandfather or grandmother, what story would you tell?

99

What are two things
you can do to improve
your health?

100

If you could write a book,
what would it be about?

101

How many of the fifty
states have you visited?

102

How many state capitals
have you visited?

103

What does it mean that
God is love?

104

How can the Catholic church have a more positive influence in Hollywood?

105

What are your thoughts
on the Sacrament of
Healing (Reconciliation)?

106

How does God speak to you through nature?

107

Which sin is worse, that
of *comission* or that
of *omission*?

108

What does Satan use to attack you?

109

Describe yourself in two words.

110

What's your favorite
movie? Why?

111

What's your favorite book? Why?

112

What do you remember about summer vacations when you were growing up?

113

What does it mean to suffer?

114

How often do you talk
with God?

115

How do you listen to God?

116

How are fouls in basket-
ball like sins in life?

117

How are women like
tabernacles?

118

What's the toughest
situation you've had to
deal with in your life?

119

Have you ever been
ridiculed for your faith?
How so?

120

When was the last time
someone hurt your
feelings?

121

What is your favorite dinner?

122

How is dinner time at home like the Liturgy of the Eucharist?

123

After Jesus forgave the sinner, He began writing in the sand while the accusers departed. What do you think Jesus was writing?

124

Should the United States have been involved in Vietnam? Why or why not?

125

When does life begin?

126

How does your family
celebrate Christmas?

127

What makes you different
from everyone else?

128

How does your family
celebrate Easter?

129

How can you use the season of Lent to prune yourself to bear better fruit?

130

What song accurately describes your life right now?

131

Who was your favorite teacher in elementary school? Why?

132

Should children get paid
to do chores at home?
Why or why not?

133

How much, if anything, should a child get for an allowance?

134

What was your favorite
subject in high school
and why?

135

Are professional athletes today overpaid? Why or why not?

136

What does it mean to
be a Christian? to be a
Catholic?

137

Why do some folks
believe that Catholics
are not Christians?

138

Was it right to drop
the atomic bomb on
Hiroshima and Nagasaki
in World War II?

139

Which recent movie have you seen that depicts the Catholic church in a positive light?

140

You are trapped on a deserted island, and you can have three items. What items would you select?

141

Why do some folks choose
to not be Catholic?

142

If you could be a character from any book, which character would you be?

143

Which is worse, to murder or to steal? Why?

144

In John 6, what does Christ mean when he says "whoever eats my flesh and drinks my blood has eternal life"?

145

What's the worst movie
you've ever seen and why?

146

How has birth control influenced divorce in this country?

147

Are you more of an
introvert or an extrovert?

148

What's a funny memory
from high school?

149

If the Vatican called you today and enabled you to ask the Pope a question, what would you ask?

150

What compact disc is in
your stereo at this time?

151

When do you prefer to go to Mass?

152

What makes America a
great nation?

153

What is your approach to Lent?

154

Do you prefer to live in
the city or country? Why?

155

Do you know someone
who has had an abortion?
What can you share about
their experience?

156

Which is the worst of
the Ten Commandments
to break?

157

Which one of the Ten
Commandments do teens
struggle with the most?

158

---•---

Which one of the Ten
Commandments do
married folks struggle
with the most?

159

Which one of the Ten Commandments do retired folks struggle with the most?

160

Which gift of the Holy Spirit would you like most at this time in your life?

161

What does this statement mean to you: Jesus, I trust in you!

162

Why is family important?

163

What would you have at your funeral that would be different than any other?

164

How are weddings opportunities for evangelization?

165

How are funerals opportunities for evangelization?

166

If you could change one thing about yourself, what would you change?

167

If your child wanted to enter the religious life, what would you tell him or her?

168

How would you invite someone to Mass with you?

169

What comes to your mind
when you hear the song
Amazing Grace?

170

What are the pros and
cons of television?

171

How do you handle
temptation?

172

Who is your best friend and why?

173

How has marriage
changed in America
since World War II?

174

If you could serve your country, which branch of service would you choose? Why that branch?

175

How would you go about
eliminating pornography
on the Internet?

176

Should the Confederate flag be allowed on state flags? Why or why not?

177

Do you play the lottery?

178

What does "safe sex" mean to you?

179

What's the funniest clean
joke that you know?

180

Who is your favorite aunt and why?

181

Who is your favorite
uncle and why?

182

---◆---

If you could ask Hollywood one question, what would you ask?

183

Which vow would be most difficult for you to keep; poverty, chastity, or obedience?

184

Do you prefer the mountains or the beach? Why?

185

How would you explain Pope John Paul II's Theology of the Body?

186

Which of the Twelve Apostles can you relate to the most?

187

During road trips, what do you do to pass the time?

188

Should women be allowed to be priests? Why or why not?

189

If you could learn more about one issue in the Catholic church, what would that issue be?

190

Why should people dress modestly?

191

What will you remember
most about Pope John
Paul II's papacy?

192

Have you ever been to the Vatican or know someone who has? What was it like?

193

How do you keep things
balanced in your life?

194

Tell about the person
who taught you to pray
the Rosary.

195

Why is there so much
violence in today's music?

196

Which religious order do you connect with most and why?

197

Should pornography be
legal? Why or why not?

198

What does it mean that "sex sells"?

199

How do you guard your heart?

200

Why do people fall away
from the Catholic church?

201

Do you think Judas Iscariot went to heaven or hell? Why?

202

If Adolph Hitler repented of his sins before he died, should he go to heaven or hell? Why?

203

Who are your heroes?

204

Do you have any nick-
names and how did you
get them?

205

How can sports be used
to evangelize?

206

How can the church
recover from the sexual
abuse scandals?

207

What does it mean to *propose* instead of *impose* with regards to sharing your faith?

208

If faith were a food, which food would it be?

209

Where do you stand on
gun control?

210

When it comes to money, what are your thoughts on how to spend and save?

211

How do you know when something is right or wrong?

212

To you, what does this sentence mean: "The family that prays together, stays together"?

213

What are issues that get
you on your soapbox?

214

How does your family
deal with death?

215

What is the right way
to deal with terrorism
around the world?

216

If there was a fire in your house, which item would you want to save and why?

217

How much is enough?

218

---◆---

Which Station of the
Cross can you relate
to most at this time in
your life?

219

If the Pope became too sick, should he step down to allow a new pope to be elected?

220

What's your favorite
number and why?

221

---◆---

What's the most beautiful
thing you have ever seen?

222

How do you define
attractive?

223

If your child came home
and announced he/she
was getting a tattoo, how
would you handle the
situation?

224

How many, if any, body
piercings are too many?

225

Is it more important to have a parent at home for the kids or have more money by having both parents working?

226

Should the Eucharist
be denied to Catholic
politicians who support
abortion?

227

Should there be adult catechism or Sunday school classes for adults? Would you attend if they were available to you?

228

---◆---

Why is euthanasia wrong
for people but okay for
animals?

229

How do you respond when non-Catholics ask why they cannot participate in our Eucharist? Do you think we should be more inclusive or less?

230

How do you handle the issue of homosexuality? Is there a difference in how you feel about the issue and how you treat homosexual individuals? Should there be?

231

How much censoship
(i.e. searching their
rooms, monitoring email
and Internet use, etc.) do
you think is appropriate
by parents of teenagers?

232

What does the Sacrament of Confirmation mean to you? Is it something you do or something God does to you?

233

Have you ever had to have a pet put down (put to sleep)? Can you share the experience?

234

If you could choose any pet, what would it be? What would you name it? Would it stay indoors or outdoors?

235

How do you squeeze
toothpaste from a tube?

236

If you won a free two-week vacation to anywhere in the world, where would you choose to travel?

237

What is your favorite season and why?

238

What thoughts go through your mind when you encounter someone who is severely disabled, either mentally or physically, or both?

239

How do you feel about making the sign of the cross in public places?

240

What are your feelings when you discover that someone you work with or go to school with is Catholic?

241

Who is the closest
person to you who has
died? What was your
experience of that death?

242

How do you feel about
donating blood?

243

Which question in this book really pushes your buttons?

ABOUT THE AUTHOR

———— • ————

Brimming with energy, a very quick wit, and a passion for living the authentic life, Dominic Catalano brings excitement, humor, and purpose to Catholic evangelism. A central Florida native, Dominic served in the United States Coast Guard and traveled the world for over eleven years before returning home. Since 1997, he has ministered to all ages, especially youth and young adults, throughout the country. Currently he is CEO of CATgear, a Catholic clothing company (www.eCATgear.com), and an avid basketball official. He enjoys traveling, playing sports, and spending time with family and friends.

Cookinary Arts
ISBN: 1-889465-06-2

This 400 page treasure trove of Italian recipes and more was written by my grandmother, Grandma Rosa. Like Grandma used to say, "we live so we can eat!", and this cookbook is all that and more. Perfect for weddings, graduations, and house warmings.

Don't delay, contact us today!
CATprints
Post Office Box 441
Eustis, Florida 32727-0441
352.636.8750
www.eCATgear.com

 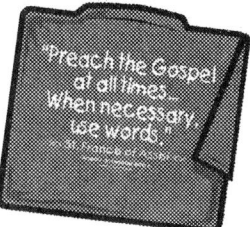

Order Information

Fax orders: **(352) 357-9211**
please use this form

Telephone orders: **(352) 636-8750**
please have your credit card ready

E-mail requests to: **Dominic@eCATgear.com**

Postal orders: **CATprints
P. O. Box 441
Eustis, Florida 32727-0441**

Please send me_____copies of QUESTIONS
FOR CATHOLICS @ $9.95 each, plus $2.00 per
book for shipping and handling domestic.

Please send more more FREE information on:
        CATprints books and products
        CATgear products

Name: _____

Address: _____

City: _____ State: ___ Zip: _____

Telephone: _____

E-mail address: _____

*sales tax: please add 7% for books shipped to Florida
addresses, thank you.*

Payment:_____ check_____visa_____mastercard

Card number:_____

Name on card:_____ exp:___/___

Signature:_____

"Dominic truly walks the talk in every aspect of his passionate faith life. He relies on his faith as a moral barometer in responding to life's challenges and brings great joy and excitement to faith discussions. This book is a reflection of his desire to know more about himself and his Catholic faith."

Maria C. Roberts
Attorney, Mother, Wife
San Diego, California

"This book is another great idea from Dominic Catalano who loves his Catholic faith with his whole being. These thought provoking questions are sure to challenge and inspire many young people to examine their own knowledge and growth in the faith, and our Church will be stronger because of this."

Mary Pat Van Epps
Director, Diocese of Memphis NFP Center
Memphis, Tennessee

"WOW! this book presents some great thought provoking questions! I am looking forward to using them to challenge myself as well as the young people with whom I minister. The unique interactive format allows all seekers of Truth to grow toward a deeper understanding of ourselves, of the world we live in, and of our faith."

Lori Seelhoff, SFO
Veterinarian and Youth Ministry Team Volunteer
Winter Park, Florida

"I believe this book will be a great ice-breaker for not only Catholics that have been born into the Catholic faith, but it's a great way to reply to the many questions of others inquiring into the Catholic faith. A book like this will be invaluable in EVERY Catholic home!"

Diann Foster
Missouri Representative
PROLIFE Across AMERICA
www.ProLifeAcrossAmerica.org
Auvasse, Missouri

"This book is an ideal instrument for helping stimulate interest in the Catholic faith. I strongly recommend this work to all youth and campus ministers."

Andrew Boyd
Student President, UCF Catholic Campus Ministry
Orlando, Florida

"Dominic provides a creative tool for small groups to use for stimulating discussions. These thought provoking and faith challenging questions invite respondents to articulate a meaning to their faith. Everyone should have this book."

Rev. Timothy P. Daly
Ormond Beach, Florida

"My wife and I enjoyed an evening of questions and answers by using this book. The format is thought provoking without being canned, predictable, or boring. We also liked the straightforwardness in presentation of real life questions. This book is a must for couples and families, and it's ideal for youth groups as it stimulates learning about self as well as the Catholic faith."

Frank Wilford
Youth Director, Glenmary Sisters
www.GlenmarySisters.org
Owensboro, Kentucky

"Dominic has given us an alternative to long and boring road trips, with these questions that will take your time together to the next level. What a great concept to help the activity to keep moving or open the avenue for great teaching moments. We will be using this on all of our trips and even when we have those extra five minutes in our catechetical sessions."

Dan McGowan
Director of Religious Education
Resurrection Catholic Church
Lakeland, Florida

"Never be afraid to question first yourself. This will open your mind to be inquisitive of others, giving you the courage and desire to delve into their world, their thoughts, and dreams, allowing a connection to be made between your soul and theirs. It works. I have found that the most successful meetings have been those in which there is something I wish to know about that person or some question within myself that I wish to have answered. So, I ask my questions with an open mind and listen to their answer…the conversation has begun and so has the relationship."

Erica Catalano
my sister, Real Estate Research Specialist
Miami, Florida

"Ask and you shall receive; seek and you shall find…As we search for answers in life, we often don't ask the right questions. Dominic Catalano has provided a solution and a roadmap by offering us the opportunity to ask some of the most provocative, compelling, and controversial questions that are absolutely crucial to effective communication in any relationship. QUESTIONS FOR CATHOLICS is a must for all truth seekers!"

Dr. Patricia Fitzgerald
Founder, Santa Monica Wellness Center
Author, The Detox Solution
Santa Monica, California

"As one who is involved in ministry formation at a Catholic Seminary, I found the questions thought provoking, as well as providing hours of stimulating discussion and reflection. Thank you Dominic for this excellent resource for youth and young adult ministry as well as small faith groups. I can't wait to pass the word!"

C. Vanessa White
Catholic Theological Union
Chicago, Illinois

"Dominic is passionate about our shared Catholic faith and is continually looking for ways to excite, educate, and challenge Catholic teens. His insight and deep love for our young adults is evidenced it each new project that he tackles. "Thank God" he is CATHOLIC. Dominic has his finger on the pulse of today's teens and opens dialogue opportunities where we as adults are able to learn from our youth. We are continually inspired and thankful that Dominic came into our lives!"

Kelly & Rona Mortensen
Peer Ministers Adult Leaders,
St. Stephen's Catholic Church
Midland, Texas

"Communication is a key to any relationship. Dominic's book helps us explore questions that will bring about excellent communication for our most important relationships. I would recommend this book to anyone and everyone! It will stir up the truths about yourself, those you care about, and the Catholic faith, and can provide a means of fun entertainment too. Great for family discussions around the dinner table, the first date, or that long road trip!"

Mike Manhardt
Founder, Family Creations
Los Angeles, California

"This book is a present, then the questions the gorgeous wrapping; you don't know what exquisite treasures you will uncover in your discussions with friends or family, but the unwrapping is half the fun! What a perfect way to find the gift in others!"

Rose Sweet
Author, Dear God, Send Me a Soul Mate;
Healing the Heartbreak of Divorce
www.RoseSweet.com
Palm Desert, California